KU-037-161

the Spirit of Football

the *Spirit of Football*

KENSINGTON WEST PRODUCTIONS

HEXHAM ENGLAND

Kensington West Productions Ltd
5 Cattle Market, Hexham, Northumberland NE46 1NJ
Tel: (01434) 609933 Fax: (01434) 600066
email: kwp@kensingtonwest.demon.co.uk
website: www.kensingtonwest.demon.co.uk

Photographs by . . . . Sportsphoto Ltd

Photographic research by . . . . Stewart Kendall

Sportsphoto project management by . . . . . Stewart Kendall

Editor . . . . Mark Scandle

Designed by . . . . Diane Ridley, Nick Ridley

Origination by . . . . Pre-Press Ltd, Hong Kong

Printing by . . . . Liang Yu Printing Ltd, Hong Kong

Frontispiece: Davor Suker celebrates after Croatia beat Germany during World Cup 98
Photograph by Richard Sellers

Title Page: A Scottish fan lets his feelings show
Photograph by Richard Sellers

Facing: Eric Cantona in familiar pose playing for Manchester United in the FA Charity Shield at
Wembley against Newcastle in 1996
Photograph by Richard Sellers

Acknowledgments: The ultimate prize, the World Cup
Photograph by Stewart Kendall

Facing: Aztek Stadium, Mexico
Photograph by Stewart Kendall

Contents: Stuart Pearce lets nothing get in his way in pursuit of the ball
Photograph by Richard Sellers

Introduction: The eyes of the world only have one focus
Photograph by Richard Sellers

All rights reserved. No part of this publication may be reproduced, stored in a retrieval system, or
transmitted in any form or by any means, electronic, mechanical, photocopying, recording or otherwise,
without the prior permission of Kensington West Productions Ltd. While every effort has been made to
ensure the accuracy of the facts and data contained in this publication, no responsibility can be accepted
by the editors, or Kensington West Productions Ltd, for errors or omissions or their consequences.

© Copyright 1998 Kensington West Productions Ltd

Contents

Acknowledgments 5

Introduction from Sportsphoto Ltd 7

Chapter One - Grass Roots 9

Chapter Two - Training and the Build Up 19

Chapter Three - The National Game 33

Chapter Four - The World Game 57

Chapter Five - Winning and Losing 79

Chapter Six - Players and Personalities 101

Chapter Seven - Fever Pitch - The Fans 123

Introduction by Sportsphoto Ltd

Yorkshire based Sportsphoto is one of Britain's largest sports photographic agencies. Established in the early eighties by Stewart Kendall, Sportsphoto has an archive of millions of images capturing the atmosphere, excitement and drama of major sporting events from around the world. The company sets itself a very high standard, which results in an enviable reputation for quality and service second to none.

National and international clients regularly commission our experienced photographers for the variety and quality of their work. Highly skilled technicians accompany the photographers to events around the world to provide a fast and reliable service to newspapers and magazines whilst the back up team in the office ensure that all our clients requirements are met on time.

Constant development in modern technology demands that Sportsphoto staff be at the forefront of any changes. We feel this enables us to keep a pace with our competitors and provide our clients with the highest quality service possible from the actual taking of the picture to its arrival on the picture desk.

Alan Shearer celebrates scoring against Germany in the Semi-Final of Euro '96
Photograph by Richard Sellers

Aspiring 'Shearers' on the parks of England
Photograph by Mark Lamb

Chapter One

Grass Roots

Above: **A young footballer catches his breath after a hard game in the mud**
Photograph by David Gadd

Right: **France's Zidane holds the World Cup trophy after scoring two goals in the final against Brazil**
Photograph by Stewart Kendall

Above: **A children's football match outside the mighty Ibrox Stadium, Glasgow**
Photograph by David Davies

Opposite: **A star of the future?**
Photographs by Stewart Kendall

Left and below: **The striking young talent is plain to see in the penalty box and the middle of the park as the youngsters learn their way**
Photographs by Stewart Kendall

Right: **Warming up before a game is so important as Lee Clark of Sunderland demonstrates**
Photograph by Richard Sellers

Does the future of the game lie with the likes of this young Middlesbrough supporter?
Photograph by Sportsphoto Ltd

England in training before another tricky away match
Photograph by Stewart Kendall

Above: **Bobby Robson directs the England training**
Photograph by Stewart Kendall

Left: **Fabrizio Ravanelli stretches out during his warm up for Middlesbrough**
Photograph by Michael Mayhew

Opposite: **David Beckham enters the World Cup stage in Marseille, as England take on Tunisia**
Photograph by Stewart Kendall

Chapter Two

Training and the build up

Left: **Glenn Hoddle and team-mate stretch before a Monaco game**
Photograph by Michael Young

Right: **Wembley, minutes before the kick-off of the 1998 Coca Cola Cup Final**
Photograph by Michael Mayhew

Barnsley fans catch up on the latest team news before the game
Photographs by David Davies

Sheffield Wednesday supporters file through the turnstiles for a mid-week game
Photographs by David Davies

Scotland players sing their hearts out during the National Anthem!
Photograph by Graham Whitby Boot

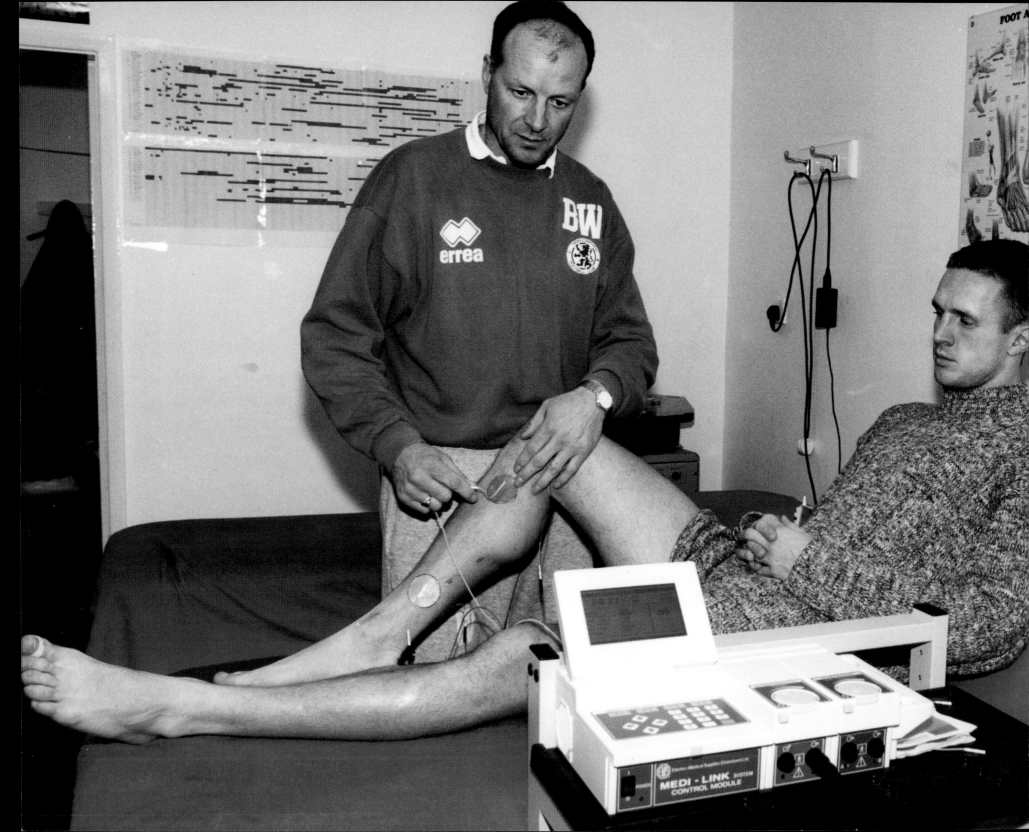

Left: **Steve Vickers of Middlesbrough on the treatment table**

Top right: **A selection of scarves to suit anyone**

Bottom right: **A programme seller enjoying brisk trade outside Oakwell, Barnsley**
Photographs by David Davies

Above: **Is the corporate market the way forward or will it kill the atmosphere of our National Game?**
Photograph by Michael Mayhew

Above: **Paul Ince trains with his Inter Milan team-mates**

Right: **Paul Ince takes on fluid after the hard work is done**
Photographs by Stewart Kendall

The preparation of a pitch starts well before the kick off
Photograph by Stewart Kendall

The England coach, Glenn Hoddle, watches his squad in training
Photograph by Paul McFegan

England's Peter Beardsley collects the balls after a hard training session
Photograph by Stewart Kendall

Steve MacMahon warms up in an unusual manner
Photograph by Stewart Kendall

Glen Hoddle and the England bench stand for the National Anthem
Photograph by Stewart Kendall

Above: **Alan Shearer takes in the atmosphere as he leads England out as captain for the first time against Moldova**
Photograph by Richard Sellers

Opposite: **Jurgen Klinsman takes a diving celebration after scoring for Tottenham**
Photograph by Stewart Kendall

Chapter Three

The National Game

Streakers of a different kind
Photograph by Michael Mayhew (left)
Photograph by David Gadd (right)

Arsenal fans celebrate at Aston Villa
Photograph by Richard Sellers

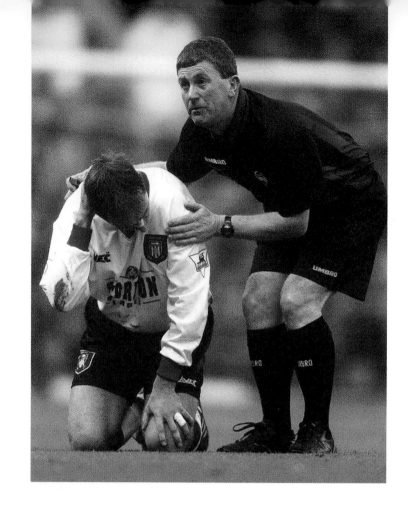

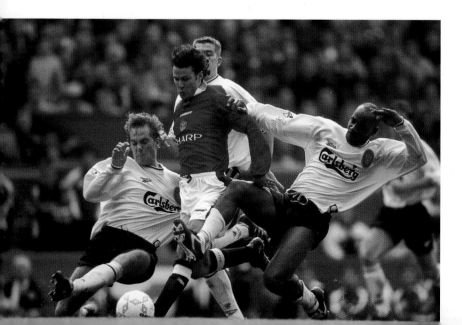

Above: **Referee Paul Durkin checks up on Sunderland's David Kelly**
Photograph by David Gadd

Left: **Ryan Giggs is tackled by Jason McAteer and Michael Thomas**
Photograph by Stewart Kendall

Right: **Everton's Danny Cadamrteri and Richard Shaw of Coventry in a 'clash of the haircuts'**
Photograph by Paul McFegan

Left: **Paul Gascoigne of Middlesbrough is tackled high and late by Chelsea's Dennis Wise in the 1998 Coca Cola Cup Final**

Right: **Peter Schmeichel screams out instructions to his defence**
Photographs by Michael Mayhew

No holds barred as Valerien of Crystal Palace plays the head instead of the ball in a tussle with Darren Huckerby of Coventry City
Photograph by Tony Edenden

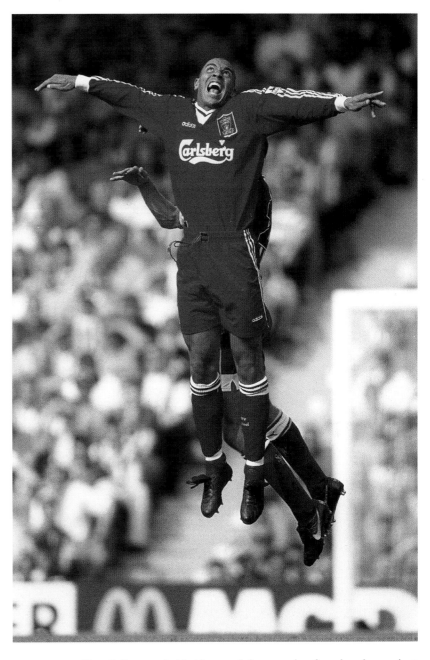

Stan Collymore in his Liverpool days soaring for a header against an opponent from Sheffield Wednesday
Photograph by Richard Sellers

Above: **Frank Clark the former Manchester City manager contemplating future prospects for the season**
Photograph by Graham Whitby Boot

Left: **Leicester's manager Martin O'Neill celebrates his team scoring**
Photograph by Tony Edenden

Right: **Everton's Duncan Ferguson and David May of Manchester United in a highly physical tussle for the ball**
Photograph by Michael Mayhew

Left: **Paul McGrath of Aston Villa climbs all over Lee Chapman of Leeds in an attempt to reach the ball**

Right: **Middlesbrough's Juninho takes five after another demanding English cup tie**
Photographs by Richard Sellers

Top left: **It's best to keep your eye on the ball as Garry Mabutt of Tottenham and Mark Hughes of Manchester United forget**
Photograph by Paul McFegan

Left: **Dennis Bergkamp of Arsenal shows sublime control against Coventry's Richard Shaw**
Photograph by Tony Edenden

Right: **Neville Southall of Everton is stretched to the limit**
Photograph by David Gadd

Gary Pallister of Manchester United is led away by his team-mate Peter Schmeichel after being incorrectly sent off against Bolton at the Reebok Stadium
Photograph by Paul McFegan

Stan Collymore celebrates scoring his first Anfield goal against Sheffield Wednesday with some uninvited Liverpool supporters
Photograph by Richard Sellers

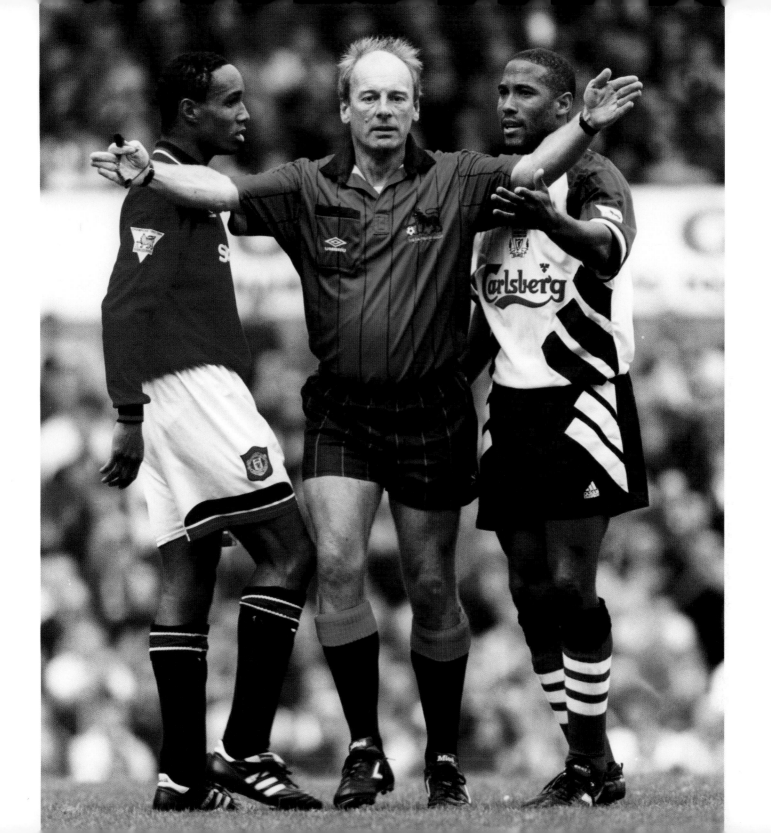

Right: **Dennis Wise of Chelsea 'cuddles' the referee in the cup tie against Grimbsy Town**
Photograph by Graham Whitby Boot

Opposite: **Which way ref? Kelvin Morton has trouble deciding whether to believe Paul Ince or John Barnes**
Photograph by Craig Thompson

Andy Hinchcliffe, playing for Everton, uses all his trickery to find a way through the Manchester United wall

Photograph by Richard Sellers

Right: **David Beckham celebrates his wonder goal from the halfway line against Wimbledon**
Photograph by Paul McFegan

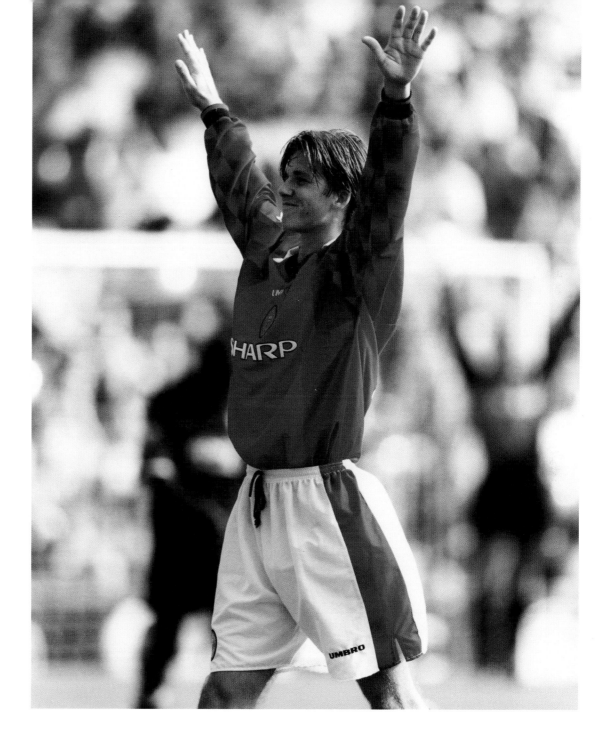

Opposite: **Fabrizio Ravanelli of Middlesbrough and Newcastle's Darren Peacock in a game of ariel ballet**
Photograph by Stewart Kendall

Right: **Newcastle's Temur Ketsbaia is brought down by Mark Draper of Aston Villa**
Photograph by Michael Mayhew

Above: **Manchester City's Fitzroy Simpson slides in for the ball on an unbelievably wet day**
Photograph by David Gadd

Paul Gascoigne of Middlesbrough and Chelsea's Eddie Newton don't know if it's football or boxing at which to ply their skills
Photograph by Michael Mayhew

Arsenal's Dennis Bergkamp leaves his mark on Newcastle's Steve Watson
Photograph by Graham Whitby Boot

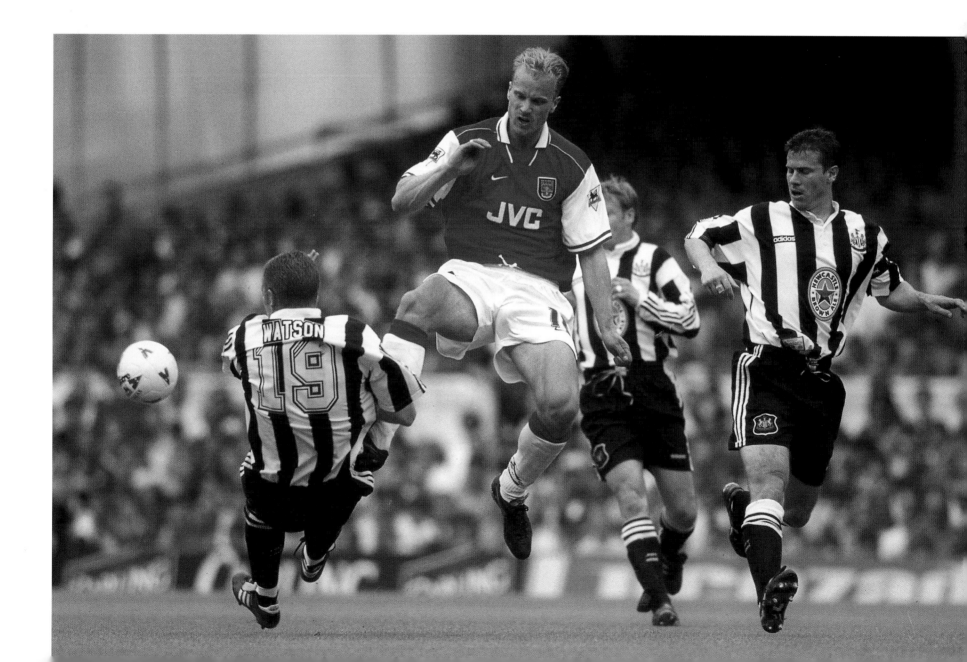

Peter Reid and the rest of the Sunderland bench strain to see the action at Barnsley
Photograph by Stewart Kendall

Right: **Croatia's Boban curls the ball over the German wall**
Photograph by Richard Sellers

Chapter Four

The World Game

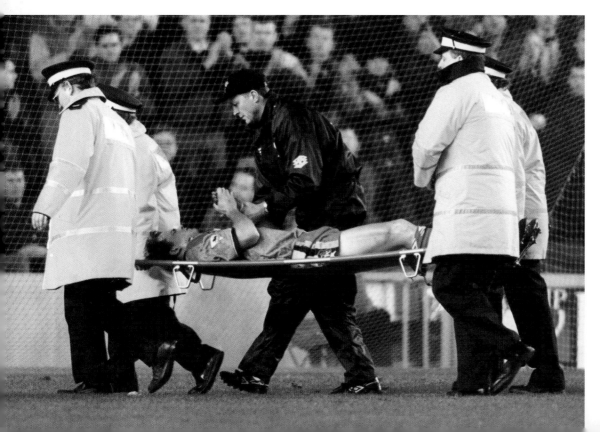

Above: **Keith Gillespie of Newcastle is stretchered off during the game against Sheffield Wednesday**
Photograph by Graham Whitby Boot

Left: **Jakob Kjeldbjerg of Chelsea is taken off the pitch with an injured wrist**
Photograph by David Gadd

Above: **Ally McCoist of Rangers is stretchered off the pitch
to discover he'll be out of action for the next three weeks**
Photograph by Graham Whitby Boot

Right: **John Pembridge of Leeds is carried off during the
match against Aston Villa**
Photograph by Stewart Kendall

Top left: **Floral tributes for Matthew Harding outside Stamford Bridge**
Photograph by Paul McFegan

Top right: **Never to be forgotten: Manchester United's tribute to their greatest manager after his death in 1994**
Photograph by David Gadd

Bottom: **Flowers are laid in memory of Matthew Harding at Stamford Bridge**
Photograph by Paul McFegan

The carnival atmosphere of the opening ceremony at the Stade De France
Photograph by David Davies

Below: **An international match for England's women's team**
Photograph by Stewart Kendall

Left: **Stuart Pearce leaves yet another opponent writhing on the floor in agony after a strong challenge**
Photograph by Richard Sellers

Right: **A German defender trying to spot that special angle the rest may have missed**
Photograph by Richard Sellers

Above: **David Seaman trying to stop a penalty in the shoot out against Germany during Euro '96**
Photograph by Richard Sellers

Left: **Hugo Sanchez of Mexico performing his customary overhead kick**
Photograph by Richard Sellers

Right: **Wembley Stadium**
Photograph by Paul McFegan

Keepers of a different style: Jorge Campos of Mexico and Peter Shilton of England collecting his award for breaking the all time English cap record
Photograph by Richard Sellers (left)
Photograph by Stewart Kendall (right)

The Republic of Ireland bench celebrate after a victory in the Euro'88 championships
Photograph by Stewart Kendall

Ronaldo and Brazil line up for the national anthems
Photograph by Stewart Kendall

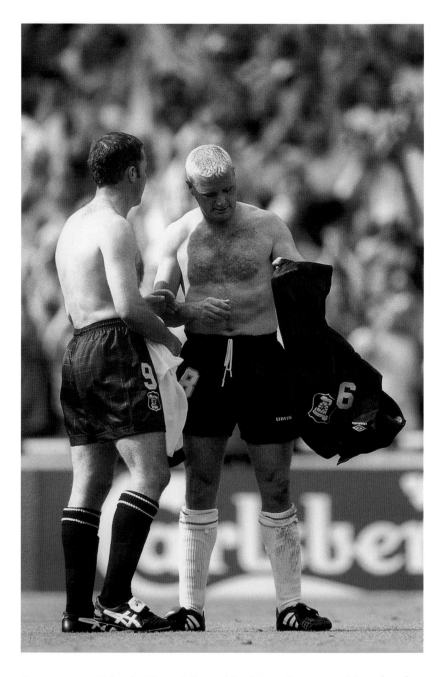

Opponents and friends Ally McCoist and Paul Gascoigne swap shirts after the England/Scotland match in Euro'96
Photograph by Richard Sellers

**Graham Taylor and the England bench contemplate the
repercussions of not qualifying for USA 94**
Photograph by Stewart Kendall

Left: **Glen Hoddle and the England coaching staff celebrate qualification for France '98**

Right: **The French physio sprays the injured ankle of one of his players in Le Tournoi**
Photographs by Stewart Kendall

Celtic fans
Photograph by Stewart Kendall

Glenn Hoddle and John Gorman look on into the sun
Photograph by Michael Mayhew

Colin Calderwood of Scotland playing a different kind of ball game
Photograph by Stewart Kendall

Raith Rovers's Scott Thompson trying to catch 'the ball'
Photograph by Richard Sellers

Another report to write up for referee Krug Hellmut
Photograph by Richard Sellers

Vinny Jones sees that familiar sight of the red card playing for Wales
Photograph by Paul McFegan

England's then player Glenn Hoddle performs an overhead kick perfectly
Photograph by Stewart Kendall

Peter Beardsley takes a heavy tumble
Photograph by Stewart Kendall

David Seaman attends to the injured Gordon Durie during the Euro '96 tournament
Photograph by Richard Sellers

Right: **Another collection of Rangers league trophies**
Photograph by Michael Mayhew

Chapter Five

Winning & Losing

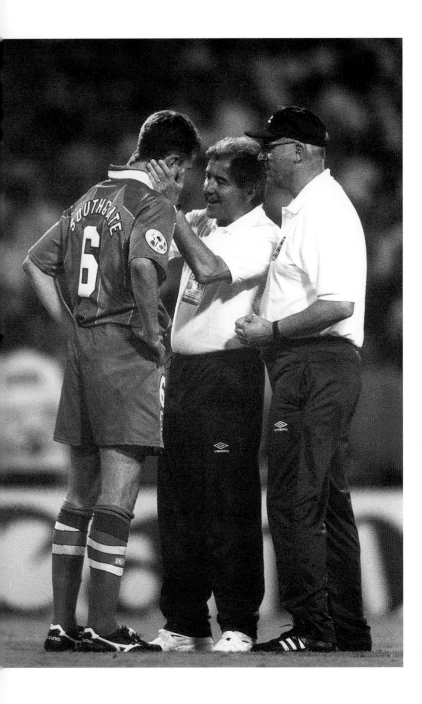

Left: **Gareth Southgate is comforted by his manager
Terry Venables after missing the final penalty in the
Semi-Final, Euro '96**

Right: **David Seaman celebrates after saving a penalty
from Spain's Miguel Angel Nadal in the Euro '96
Quarter-Final penalty shoot-out**
Photographs by Richard Sellers

Germany's Oliver Bierhoff scores the golden goal in the Euro'96 Cup Final
Photograph by Richard Sellers

**The Italian team celebrate after scoring
against the Czech Republic in Euro '96**
Photograph by Paul McFegan

Kenny Dalglish, Graeme Souness and Alan Hansen of Liverpool celebrate yet another trophy
Photograph by Stewart Kendall

Above: **Italian players suffering after their loss to Brazil in the USA 94 World Cup Final**

Left: **Dunga and Romario of Brazil celebrate with the treasured prize of the World Cup**
Photographs by Stewart Kendall

Far left: **Grim realisation dawns on Kevin Keegan and the Newcastle bench in 1996 that the Premiership would be heading to Old Trafford as another game slips away**
Photograph by Stewart Kendall

Left: **Manchester United's goalkeeper, Peter Schmeichel holds onto the ball under extreme pressure from Blackburn's Colin Hendry**
Photograph by Stewart Kendall

Left: **The final whistle blows on Scotland's adventure in Euro '96 and after giving their all, the players find it hard to bear**

Below: **Franco Baresi sits and prays during the penalty shoot-out in the USA '94 World Cup Final**

Right: **The England players celebrate amongst the massed ranks of the press after their qualification for France '98**

Photographs by Stewart Kendall

Argentina's Claudio Caniggia scores against Nigeria
Photograph by Richard Sellers

**Denmark's goalkeeper Morgens Krogh and Kevin Gallagher of Scotland try a
game of 'twister' during a match**
Photograph by Michael Mayhew

Above: **The Spanish national team celebrate after scoring**
Photograph by Stewart Kendall

Left: **Juninho and his Athletico Madrid team-mates celebrate**
Photograph by David Gadd

Right: **Football can be a lonely game as Alan Ball found out on the bench at Manchester City**
Photograph by Stewart Kendall

Below: **Chelsea's Kevin Hitchcock doesn't know where to put himself after Liverpool score their fifth goal at Anfield**
Photograph by Richard Sellers

Left: **Dunga the Brazilian Captain and a very young Ronaldo show off the nice new trophy they've just won**
Photograph by Stewart Kendall

Far left: **Shearer and Ince await the outcome of the penalty shoot-out during Euro '96**
Photograph by Michael Mayhew

Above: **Stuart Pearce scores his penalty at Wembley in Euro 96 and doing so exorcises the ghost of the World Cup '90**

Right: **Paul Gascoigne does his 'dentist chair trick' with Teddy Sheringham after his memorable goal against Scotland at Wembley in Euro 96**
Photographs by Richard Sellers

Left: **Fabrizio Ravanelli's trademark celebration after scoring**
Photograph by Michael Mayhew

Below: **Frank Sinclair celebrates in an unusual manner**
Photograph by Andy Blackwell

Far left: **England's Alan Shearer basks in the glory of his goal against Scotland in Euro '96**
Photograph by Richard Sellers

Beckham, Ince and Gascoigne celebrate their victory in Italy
Photograph by Nigel Acklam

Opposite: **Ian Wright, Arsenal**
Photograph by Richard Sellers

Chapter Six

Players & Personalities

Far left: **Diego Maradona**
Photograph by Michael Mayhew

Left: **The face that inspires millions;
Brazil's Ronaldo during USA '94**
Photograph by Stewart Kendall

Brian Clough, as usual never far from controversy
Photograph by Mark Liley

Conflicting views between George Graham the manager of Leeds and Alex Ferguson of Manchester United
Photograph by Graham Whitby Boot

Top: **Ireland's manager Jack Charlton just can't bear to watch**
Photograph by Stewart Kendall

Bottom: **Ken Bailey in his usual outfit for England**
Photograph by Stewart Kendall

Left **Eric Cantona in a familiar pose**
Photograph by: Richard Sellers

Right: **Maybe the best of all time: George Best rolls back the years with a performance to excite the fans**
Photograph by Stewart Kendall

Paul Gascoigne shows his cheek with a prank on Paul Ince
Photograph by Stewart Kendall

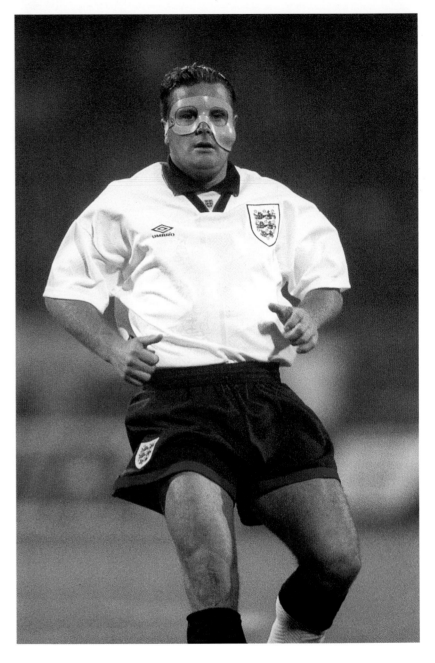

Paul Gascoigne wearing his protective face mask for a fractured cheek-bone
Photograph by Richard Sellers

Marco Van Baston-AC Milan
Photograph by Stewart Kendall

Above: **Mark Hughes of Manchester United lies injured on the grass after being clattered from behind**
Photograph by Stewart Kendall

Top left: **No matter who you play for, when you get injured the feeling is always the same as players from Manchester United and Feyernoord show**
Photograph by Richard Sellers

Left: **Ray Wilkins of QPR is floored by Neil Morrissey of Tranmere**
Photograph by Graham Whitby Boot

Above: **Scotland's Colin Hendry lies injured**

Left: **Ed De Goey of Feyernoord receives treatment during a game against Everton**
Photographs by Richard Sellers

Kevin Keegan, the old Newcastle idol
Photograph by Richard Sellers

Celtic's Di Canio shows his emotions
Photograph by Paul McFegan

Paul Gascoigne celebrates in an inappropriate manner
Photograph by Richard Sellers

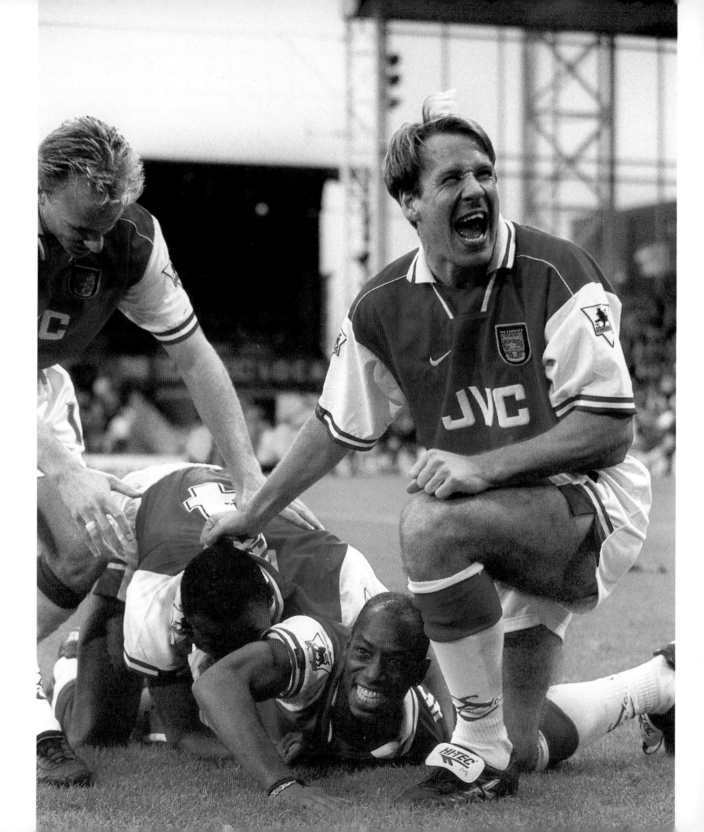

Ian Wright, the Highbury idol, after scoring 'again'
Photograph by Graham Whitby Boot

Ian Rush throws his shirt into the Kop after his final appearance for Liverpool
Photograph by Ronnie Hayward

Left & Below: **The two sides of Eric Cantona; rejoicing with the crowd at Old Trafford and complaining to the referee after a decision goes against him**
Photograph by Paul McFegan
Photograph by Richard Sellers

Right: **Alan Shearer, then of Blackburn, controlling the ball against his current team Newcastle**
Photograph by Richard Sellers

Left: Liverpool's Phil Babb and Jurgen Klinsman of Tottenham chase the ball
Photograph by Richard Sellers

Right: Poalo Di Canio of Sheffield Wednesday and Vialli of Chelsea talking Italian
Photograph by Michael Mayhew

Bottom right: David Ginola is stopped in full flight
Photograph by Michael Mayhew

Bottom left: Juninho celebrates with a Middlesbrough supporter
Photograph by Michael Mayhew

Dennis Bergkamp battles with Gary Neville in an 'all Premiership' international battle
Photograph by Richard Sellers

Left: **Celtic's Cadete and Di Canio celebrate Cadete's goal against Kilmarnock**
Photograph by David Gadd

Below: **Matthew Le Tissier of Southampton covers Blackburn's Tim Flowers after a trademark save**
Photograph by Graham Whitby Boot

Far right: **Ruud Gullit continues the reputation of exceptional Dutch Number 10s**
Photograph by Richard Sellers

Bottom right: **The most famous number 10 of all, praying for the hand of God? Again?**
Photograph by Richard Sellers

David Seaman asks, is there anybody out there?
Photograph by Richard Sellers

Opposite: **Fanatical fans at Sampadoria in Italy**
Photograph by Sportsphoto Ltd

Chapter Seven

The Fans

Left: **Blackburn fans celebrating the goal in their own way**
Photograph by Stewart Kendall

Above: **Paul Gregory, known as Tango man, cheers on his side Sheffield Wednesday**
Photograph by Stewart Kendall

Opposite:

Bottom right: **The queues keep on growing outside the Manchester United superstore**
Photograph by Stewart Kendall

Top right: **Swedish fans**
Photograph by Tony Edenden

Left: **A Scottish fan at Euro '96**
Photograph by Richard Sellers

Above: **A Dutch supporter wearing his colours**
Photograph by Richard Sellers

Right: **Brazillian supporters take a time out during USA'94**
Photograph by Stewart Kendall

Far left: **German football fans**
Photograph by Richard Sellers

Left: **A Mexican fan at USA '94**
Photograph by Richard Sellers

Bottom left: **Danish Fans**
Photograph by Stewart Kendall

Bottom right: **Dutch and Scottish fans**
Photograph by Stewart Kendall

Left: **A Swedish fan shows his colours**
Photograph by Richard Sellers

Above: **A Brazilian fan blows his trumpet**
Photograph by Stewart Kendall

Top left: **Police with their dogs patrolling the crowds**
Photograph by Stewart Kendall

Bottom left: **English hooligans throw debris during the England v Republic of Ireland friendly match**
Photograph by Tony Edenden

Right: **England fans appeal to the Italian police who had led a baton charge into the travelling supporters**
Photograph by Stewart Kendall

Left: **England fans cheer on their side**
Photograph by Paul McFegan

Above: **A Scottish crowd at Wembley**
Photograph by Richard Sellers

Right: **Celtic fans after the best view of the day**
Photograph by Steve Morton

Top: **Argentinian fans**
Photograph by Stewart Kendall

Left: **Hearts fans look on in the pouring rain against their local rivals Hibernian**
Photograph by Graham Whitby Boot

Opposite page:

Bottom left: **The Stadium of Light, Sunderland**
Photograph by David Gadd

Top right: **A Saudi Arabian fan gets his message over in a rather loud manner**
Photograph by Richard Sellers

Top left: **Colombian fans make their message clear and simple**
Photograph by Richard Sellers

Bottom right: **Italian fans**
Photograph by Richard Sellers

Top: **AC Milan fans let off flares**

Bottom: **Supporters from Fiorentina ask a strange question**

Far Right: **Italian Fans**
Photographs by Richard Sellers

Left: **Newcastle fans show their feelings on Keegan's decision to quit**
Photograph by Paul McFegan

Far left: **An AC Milan fan holds on tight**
Photograph by Tony Edenden

Dutch fans during the World Cup USA '94
Photograph by Richard Sellers

Bologna fans watching a game in the rain
Photograph by Graham Whitby Boot

Irish celebrations
Photograph by Stewart Kendall

Barnsley fans celebrate promotion
Photograph by Paul McFegan

The Spirit of

Above: **Dutch fans at Wembley**
Photographs by Tony Edenden

Left: **An Eric Cantona caricature**
Photographs by Tony Edenden

Above: **An England fan cheers his side to victory at Wembley**
Photograph by Paul McFegan

Right: **A flag salesman sets out his stall**
Photograph by Mark Liley

...inst Germany
.endall